21st
Century
Skills Library

REAL WORLD MATH: GEOGRAPHY

PLAINS AND PLATEAUS

BY BARBARA A. SOMERVILL

CHERRY LAKE Publishing

Published in the United States of America by
Cherry Lake Publishing, Ann Arbor, Michigan
www.cherrylakepublishing.com

Content Adviser
Andrew Dombard, Associate Professor, Department of Earth and Environmental
Sciences, University of Illinois at Chicago
Math Adviser: Tonya Walker, MA, Boston University

Credits
Photos: Cover and page 1, ©iStockphoto.com/4loops; page 4, ©Photoaged/
Dreamstime.com; page 6, ©javarman, used under license from Shutterstock, Inc.;
page 8, ©BigBen0123/Dreamstime.com; page 10, ©Deviousrim/Dreamstime.com;
page 13, ©Isselee/Dreamstime.com; page 14, ©Taolmor/Dreamstime.com; page 15,
©Maria Dryfhout, used under license from Shutterstock, Inc.; page 16, © Arco
Images GmbH / Alamy; page 18, ©Jakeblaster/Dreamstime.com; page 21,
©Poutnik/Dreamstime.com; page 22, ©Fallsview/Dreamstime.com; page 25,
©Neil Wigmore, used under license from Shutterstock, Inc.; page 26, ©mycola,
used under license from Shutterstock, Inc.

Library of Congress Cataloging-in-Publication Data
Somervill, Barbara A.
 Plains and plateaus / by Barbara A. Somervill.
    p. cm.—(Real world math: geography)
 Includes index.
 ISBN-13: 978-1-60279-493-1
 ISBN-10: 1-60279-493-6
 1. Plains—Juvenile literature. 2. Plateaus—Juvenile literature. I. Title.
II. Series.
 GB571.S66 2009
 577.4—dc22   2008048298 I

Cherry Lake Publishing would like to acknowledge
the work of The Partnership for 21st Century Skills.
Please visit *www.21stcenturyskills.org* for more information.

TABLE OF CONTENTS

CHAPTER ONE
WHAT ARE PLAINS AND PLATEAUS?

Plains are broad, open lands. The land appears flat with low, rolling hills. Many plains are grasslands. The area is often covered with wild grasses. But grasses aren't the only plants

The many different plants growing in grasslands often makes the landscape very colorful.

that grow in grasslands. Mixed in with the grass are sedges, rushes, reeds, and wildflowers.

Plains have deep soil deposits. Millions of years ago, oceans or seas covered many of today's plains regions. The oceans eventually disappeared, leaving behind **sediment**. In some places, sediment is miles deep. Some of the sediment makes the soil rich and fertile. This soil makes plains regions good for farming.

Plains are found on every continent. In North America, plains are called prairies. Prairies cover the central portion of Canada and the United States. This area is sometimes called the Great Plains. The Great Plains has three types of prairie: tallgrass, mixed-grass, and short-grass.

REAL WORLD MATH CHALLENGE

In 1862, the United States Congress passed the Homestead Act. This law allowed people to claim land on the Great Plains for farming. On January 1, 1863, a total of 418 people filed claims for 160 acres of land each. **How many acres of land did these settlers claim?**

(Turn to page 29 for the answer)

Savannas are tropical grasslands. They usually feature widely spaced, low trees. They are found in Australia, Africa, and South America. Savannas have two major seasons. The wet season brings heavy rainfall. The grass becomes thick and green. The dry season is long. Months without rainfall cause savanna grasses to dry up. But when the rains come, the grasses grow again.

A steppe is another type of grassland. Short-grass prairie could be considered a steppe. Steppes are drier and colder than most grasslands. Steppes are found in Russia, Mongolia, and Kazakhstan.

During the dry season, the savannah can look almost like a desert.

LIFE & CAREER SKILLS

You may have heard news reports of wildfires that put people in danger and cause millions of dollars in property damage. But did you know that fires can help an **ecosystem** stay healthy? Scientists have realized that wildfires are a natural part of plains **ecology**. Wildfires clear dead plant matter and put **nutrients** back into the soil. More sunlight can reach the soil, too. Fire encourages new growth.

Authorities may use fire to control the plant growth in prairies. They work together as a team. Their cooperation is important. Fires must be closely monitored and managed. Why do you think experts work hard to make sure that any fires stay within established borders?

Some steppes are found on plateaus. Plateaus are flat, raised lands. They can also be called tablelands. Plateaus can be small and part of a larger plains region. The Missouri Plateau, for example, is a plateau that is part of the Great Plains.

Plateaus are formed by interesting geological events. When two landmasses strike each other, the land is forced to move upward. Sometimes, these geological events form mountains.

Plateaus cover about 45 percent of Earth's land surface. One of the largest plateaus is the Tibetan Plateau. The Tibetan Plateau rises 13,123 to 16,404 feet (4,000 to 5,000 meters) above sea level. China's major rivers start in lakes on the Tibetan Plateau. The land seems harsh, bare, and cold, but there is plenty of plant and animal life.

On the other side of the Himalaya Mountains, the Deccan Plateau is the largest plateau in India. The land is lush, green,

Napahai Lake is on the Tibetan Plateau. In the fall and winter the lake dries out, making it perfect for grazing animals!

and covered with forest. Unlike the Tibetan Plateau, the Deccan Plateau is heavily populated. Many of the people are farmers who produce cotton, sugarcane, rice, and vegetables.

Plateaus made mainly of sedimentary rock suffer from **erosion**. Water and wind carve plateau rocks into strange, unusual shapes. The rock formations may be buttes, hoodoos, goblins, and arches. Buttes are isolated hills that rise up on a plateau. Hoodoos are odd-shaped pillars that remain after all the rock around them is worn away. Goblins are made of sandstone. They are short and mushroom shaped. Arches are naturally formed bridges.

REAL WORLD MATH CHALLENGE

In 1,000 years, a fast-running river might erode 5 centimeters of sedimentary rock. **How many years does it take to erode 1 cm of rock? How long might it take for a river to erode 30 cm of rock?**

(Turn to page 29 for the answers)

CHAPTER TWO
ALL ABOUT GRASS

You come into contact with grasses—in one form or another—more than you might think. You've seen the mowed grass that grows on lawns. You also eat grass. No, you don't

Wild grasses are often considered weeds. Homeowners work to keep them out of their lawns.

eat the stuff that grows on a soccer field. You eat grains, which are grass seeds. Wheat, oats, wild rice, rye, and millet come from grains. These crops originally grew wild on grassy plains.

Every grasslands region has its own varieties of grass. There are approximately 10,000 species of grass. No grasslands region has just one grass species. Dozens of species grow together. But every grassland has two or three main grass species.

Two hundred years ago, open prairie covered the Great Plains. Tallgrass prairie thrived in the east. Common grasses of a tallgrass prairie were big bluestem, Indian grass, and prairie cordgrass. These grasses grew up to 10 feet (3 m) tall. Short-grass prairie lay to the west. Common grasses of a short-grass prairie were buffalo grass and little bluestem. Mixed-grass prairie is found in between tallgrass and short-grass prairies. It features patches of tall and short-grass species.

REAL WORLD MATH CHALLENGE

A cluster of Indian grass measures 120 centimeters tall. The roots have grown 180 centimeters below the surface. **What is the total length of the plant? What percent of the plant is above ground?**

(Turn to page 29 for the answers)

Many settlers thought clearing prairie for farming would be easy. After all, they would not have to cut down trees. Those settlers were wrong. The grass seen aboveground equals about one-third the total mass of the plant. Grassland root systems are dense and strong. They may reach 10 to 13 feet

21ST CENTURY CONTENT

In 1951, Serengeti National Park was established in Tanzania, Africa. The park extends over approximately 5,700 square miles (14,763 square km). The area could have been turned into farmland. But Tanzania's officials had a different vision. This park serves as a spectacular wildlife preserve. It features elephants, zebras, giraffes, lions, cheetahs, leopards, and wildebeest. Hundreds of bird species make Serengeti their home.

But wildlife in Serengeti isn't totally safe. Thousands of animals are killed illegally every year for their meat. The government, park officials, and local communities will have to work together to solve this problem. The security of the park is worth the effort. It is the only place in Africa where seasonal migrations of certain animals still occur.

Zebras are just one of the many kinds of animals that live on the Serengeti plain.

(3 to 4 m) deep. Hacking through the thick tangle of roots was backbreaking work.

Grasslands on other continents have different grass species. Australia has spear grass and many other species. Africa's Serengeti plains feature dropseed grasses and other varieties.

Different grasses grow in different climates. Drier grasslands have short-grass that needs very little water.

In Indonesia, farmers grow rice in rice fields. The land is so wet, farmers can grow three or more crops each year!

People walking through tallgrass prairies should be on the lookout for snakes.

Wild rice and wild ryegrasses prefer wetlands. They need more water to live. They sprout up by rivers and ponds.

The grasses that grow in plains regions determine which animals can live there. Animals that graze on grasses need to be able to see when **predators** approach. Wildebeest, antelopes, and zebras of the Serengeti roam among short-grasses. Tallgrass prairie is ideal for animals that need a good place to hide. Such animals include deer, snakes, badgers, and certain birds, such as quail and pheasants.

CHAPTER THREE
DO THE MATH: CLIMATE

Plains enjoy a fairly dry, **temperate** climate. **Precipitation** ranges from 8 inches (20 cm) to 40 inches (102 cm) per year. The precipitation patterns keep the grasslands grassy. Trees need plenty of water on a regular basis. In most grasslands, dry periods last too long for trees to survive.

Snow can make it difficult for bison and other prairie animals to find food.

Temperatures can range from winter lows of 32° Fahrenheit (0° Celsius) or colder to sweltering summer days. It is not unusual to find summertime temperatures pushing 104° F (40°C).

In the savannas, precipitation comes as rain. Savannas do not have four seasons. Instead, they have a wet season and a dry season. The Serengeti Plain is a good example. This region is near the equator, so the temperatures are fairly warm all year long. From June to November, hardly any rain falls at all. The grass dries up and begins to look like straw.

Most of the area's yearly rainfall occurs from late March through May. The earth is renewed. Lush grass grows to feed the millions of plant eaters that live on the Serengeti Plain.

During the dry season, the soil becomes hard as rock. When heavy rains fall, the soil cannot absorb so much water. The water pours into streams and rivers. The water level rises and spreads over the riverbanks. In this way, heavy rains can cause serious flooding.

On steppes and prairies, precipitation can fall in the form of rain, snow, hail, or sleet. These plains areas have four definite seasons. Winters can be extremely cold and snowy. At least one blizzard a year blankets the land in snow.

The spring and fall bring mild temperatures and moderate rainfall. The prairie has dramatic thunder and lightning storms.

People on the Great Plains face a serious threat from tornadoes. About 1,200 tornadoes whip across the Great

Plains every year. That is more than anywhere else in the world. April, May, and June experience the most tornadoes. Severe tornadoes are destructive storms. They can destroy everything in their path.

Some plateaus that are part of grasslands share the same climate as the grasslands. The climate on high plateaus, however, can be very different. Examples of regions with plateau climate zones are the Tibetan Plateau and the Colorado Plateau.

"Tornado Alley" is the name given to the central U.S. region where many tornadoes form.

REAL WORLD MATH CHALLENGE

Heavy rains in Kenya feed the Mara River. In one area along the Serengeti Plain, the Mara River floods its banks when the water reaches 12 meters deep. Read the chart and answer the questions below.

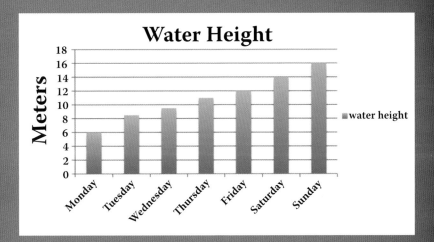

On which day did the water reach flood height? How many meters did the water level increase from Monday to Friday? How much did the river rise in one week?

(Turn to page 29 for the answers)

The **altitude** and weather of the Tibetan Plateau limit the plants and animals that can live there. Most of the plateau is treeless, except in the southeastern river valley. There are a few meadows, but much of the land looks like desert.

LEARNING & INNOVATION SKILLS

The Tibetan Plateau, like other regions around the world, is feeling the effects of global climate change. Glaciers throughout the Tibetan Plateau have been shrinking over the past several decades.

How will melting glaciers affect the plateau? Will other parts of Asia be affected, too? Scientists have to find answers to these tough questions. One way they find answers is by carefully studying various sets of data. Scientists also use special equipment such as sensors to gather information. The results worry many people. Melting glaciers could lead to flooding in some regions and drought in others. The flows of important rivers would also be affected. Further research will shed more light on how global warming could alter the climate in the region.

Parts of the Colorado Plateau are very dry. Even close to the Colorado River, the land can be harsh and arid.

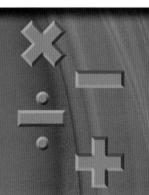

REAL WORLD MATH CHALLENGE

An area of the Colorado Plateau now has a yearly precipitation rate of 50 cm. In 1909, the precipitation rate was about 80% of what it is today. **What was the precipitation rate in 1909?**

(Turn to page 29 for the answer)

CHAPTER FOUR
DO THE MATH: BIODIVERSITY

Biodiversity includes the mix of animals and plants found in an ecosystem. A healthy ecosystem has a wide variety of animals and plants. From prairie to savanna, plains to plateau, the plant and animal populations are different. The type of available food is different. The climate changes from one ecosystem to another. These differences create habitats that support different plants and animals.

The short-grass prairie of North America stretches from New Mexico north to the Colorado–Wyoming border.

...the 1800s, hunting and fa...
...nct. People have...

Grass makes up approximately 64 percent of plant life in short-grass prairies. More than 100 plant species can live in a small patch of prairie. Blazing stars, coneflowers, sunflowers, and asters add color to the sea of grasses. Some cactus and yucca also grow well on short-grass prairie.

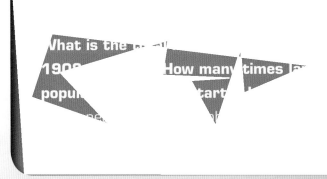

At one time, large numbers of prairie dogs built networks of homes in the ground. As they moved, the prairie dogs spread seeds and turned over soil, keeping the grass healthy. Snakes, foxes, and other animals preyed on the prairie dogs. Bison and antelope fed on the grass. Dragonflies, butterflies, and mosquitoes buzzed in the air. The insects and grass seeds fed birds, mice, and other small creatures. The short-grass prairie had a high level of biodiversity. As prairie land was lost to farming, animal and plant species struggled to survive.

21ˢᵀ CENTURY CONTENT

The llanos region is a great example of biodiversity. But the area and its wildlife are under threat. The llanos are home to one of the world's most seriously endangered reptiles: the Orinoco crocodile. The draining of wetlands, and the activities of the oil, cattle, and agricultural industries have all had a negative impact on the llanos. Finding a balance between **conservation** and industry is an important global issue in the 21st century. It's also a complicated one. Some people argue that the resources in certain areas could be used to make products and improve economies. On the other hand, many people believe it is important to protect and preserve natural habitats and wildlife. What do you think? Should companies ever be allowed to use or do business in an area where the wildlife is threatened?

The llanos of Venezuela are mixed grasslands and wetlands. This region supports many more plant and animal species than

People have been using the resources of the Orinoco River since ancient times. Tourists today visit to go canoeing and fishing.

a short-grass prairie does. There is more food available year-round. More animal species can live on the llanos. More than 3,400 different plant species thrive in the warm, wet climate.

Llanos habitats support pumas, jaguars, and other mammals. Approximately 475 types of birds live in the high plains. The Orinoco River passes through the llanos. Giant river otters and river dolphins swim in its waters.

The Tibetan Plateau is very different from the short-grass prairie or the llanos. Many of the plants and animals that live there are unique to the region. More than 5,000 species of fungi grow on the Tibetan Plateau. Mushrooms are some of the many types of fungi. Scientists have counted 12,000 species of plants. Tibetan antelopes, Bactrian camels, and wild yaks are some of the region's largest plant eaters. Although predators are few, the region does have some, such as snakes. Fish, mammals, birds, and insects are plentiful. But people are rare.

CHAPTER FIVE
CONSERVING GRASSLANDS

Throughout the world, grasslands are giving way to farms and housing developments. Roads carve the land into neat squares. Engineers dam rivers to prevent flooding and control the water supply. Waving fields of grass have become tidy rows of corn, soybeans, and winter wheat.

Long ago, tallgrass prairie covered 140 million acres (57 million hectares) in North America. Today, approximately 4 percent of natural tallgrass prairie remains. Mixed-grass and short-grass prairie have suffered the same fate. What little prairie remains is cut into small plots. Conservation groups hope to restore prairies and save the prairie ecosystem.

Wheat once grew wild on the plains. Today, farmers grow it in neat rows as crops to harvest and sell.

Prairie conservation begins with land. Today, the Canadian and U.S. governments set aside land for restoring prairies. Conservation groups, such as The Nature Conservancy, buy land to grow new prairies. Some farmers and private companies have returned some of their land to prairie, too.

 LIFE & CAREER SKILLS

Restoring a prairie is not quick or easy. There are many steps. Whatever is growing on the land must be killed. The soil should be analyzed. The roots, seeds, and bulbs of non-prairie plants must be removed. The soil needs time to rest. A prairie seed mixture is spread. But a prairie will not spring to life right away.

The process takes years. It could take years before grasses become established. Every year, the prairie will have a different mix of wildflowers and grasses.

Bringing a prairie to life takes patience and **diligence**. It takes many seasons of care and maintenance to establish plant growth. But the end result is worth the effort.

Once prairie plants are established, animal life returns. Insects and birds arrive. Birds nest among the grasses and produce young. Mice, voles, rabbits, and hares find homes. Snakes, birds of prey, and foxes arrive to feed on small prairie mammals. Eventually, white-tailed deer may find their way to restored prairie land. Little by little, nature's cycle of life will return to the open prairie. The transformation from bare soil to self-supporting prairie may take ten years or longer. Be patient! The prairie will grow again.

REAL WORLD MATH CHALLENGE

A class plans to restore prairie land to an empty nearby lot. The class considers two different prairie seed mixes. Both mixes have a blend of wildflower and grass seeds. The following chart only shows the grass seed content in each mix.

Grass Seed	Little Bluestem	Sideoats Grama	Prairie Brome	Plains Oval Sedge	Junegrass	Indian Grass
Mix One	16%	11%	4%	8%	3%	none
Mix Two	12%	10%	9%	5%	3%	6%

Which mix has a higher percentage of grass seed? Little bluestem and sideoats grama are better for a short-grass prairie. **Which mix best suits a short-grass prairie restoration? What is the percentage of wildflower seed in Mix One?**

(Turn to page 29 for the answers)

REAL WORLD MATH CHALLENGE ANSWERS

Chapter One

Page 5
The settlers claimed 66,880 acres.
418 people x 160 acres each =
66,880 acres

Page 9
It would take 200 years to erode
1 centimeter of rock.
1,000 years ÷ 5 cm = 200 years

It might take 6,000 years to erode
30 centimeters of rock.
30 cm x 200 years =
6,000 years

Chapter Two

Page 11
The total length of the plant is
300 centimeters.
120 cm + 180 cm = 300 cm

Forty percent of the plant is above
ground.
120 cm ÷ 300 cm = 0.40 = 40%

Chapter Three

Page 19
The water reached flood height on
Friday.
The water level increased 6 meters
from Monday to Friday.
Monday = 6 m
Friday = 12 m
12 – 6 = 6 meters

In one week, the river rose
10 meters.
Sunday = 16 m
Monday = 6 m
16 – 6 = 10 meters

Page 21
The precipitation rate in 1909 was
40 cm yearly.
50 x 0.80 = 40 cm

Chapter Four

Page 23
The bison population increased by
4,679 bison.
4,700 – 21 = 4,679

The bison population in 2007 is
224 times larger than the starter
population.
4,700 ÷ 21 = 223.8 = 224

Chapter Five

Page 28
Mix Two has a higher percentage of
grass seed than Mix One.
Mix One: 16 + 11 + 4 + 8 + 3 = 42%
Mix Two: 12 + 10 + 9 + 5 + 3 + 6 =
45%

Mix One is better for a short-grass
prairie restoration. Little bluestem
and sideoats grama seeds make up
27% of the mixture.
16 + 11 = 27%

Those grasses only make up 22% of
the mixture in Mix Two.
12 + 10 = 22%

Wildflower seeds make up 58% of
the mixture in Mix One. Remember
that the chart only shows the grass
seed content. This means the
remaining percentage represents
wildflower seed content.
100% – 42% grass seed = 58%
wildflower seed

GLOSSARY

altitude (AL-ti-tood) the height of something above the earth or sea level

biodiversity (bye-oh-duh-VURS-it-ee) the variety of animal and plant species in an environment

conservation (kon-sur-VAY-shuhn) the protection or preservation of animals, plants, or other things in nature

diligence (DIL-uh-juhnss) hard work

ecology (ee-KOL-uh-jee) the science that studies the relationships among plants, animals, and their surroundings

ecosystem (EE-koh-siss-tuhm) a community of living things and their environment

erosion (ee-ROH-zhuhn) the wearing away of something by wind or water

nutrients (NOO-tree-uhnts) substances in food that help animals and plants grow or live

precipitation (pri-sip-i-TAY-shuhn) the rain, sleet, hail, or snow that falls to the surface of Earth

predators (PRED-uh-turz) animals that hunt and kill other animals for food

sediment (SED-uh-muhnt) particles of rock and plant matter deposited by water, wind, or glaciers

temperate (TEM-pur-it) having to do with mild weather and temperatures that are not very high or very low

FOR MORE INFORMATION

BOOKS

Levy, Janey. *Discovering the Tropical Savanna.* New York: PowerKids Press, 2008.

Lundgren, Julie. *Grassland Buffet: Studying Food Webs in the Grasslands and Savannas.* Vero Beach, FL: Rourke Publishing, 2009.

Somervill, Barbara A. *American Bison.* Ann Arbor, MI: Cherry Lake Publishing, 2008.

WEB SITES

San Diego Zoo: Animal Bytes: Savanna
www.sandiegozoo.org/animalbytes/e-savanna.html
Find more information about savanna habitats

University of Minnesota: Build-A-Prairie
www.bellmuseum.org/distancelearning/prairie/build/index.html
Construct a prairie by choosing different plants and animals, and learn more about this interesting ecosystem

INDEX

ABOUT THE AUTHOR

Barbara Somervill loves to write about science and geography. The Real World Math series provided her with the opportunity to combine interesting facts with practical applications. Barbara has written nearly 200 children's books and school textbooks. Every book is an opportunity to learn about new and different subjects. She is married, a mother, and a grandmother, and she lives in South Carolina.